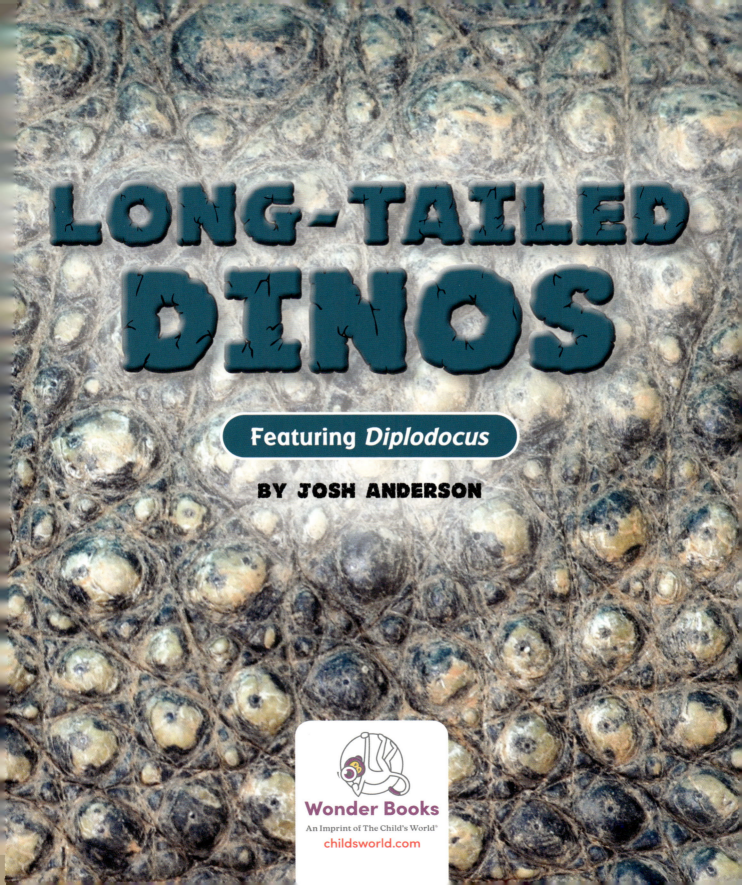

LONG-TAILED DINOS

Featuring *Diplodocus*

BY JOSH ANDERSON

Wonder Books
An Imprint of The Child's World®
childsworld.com

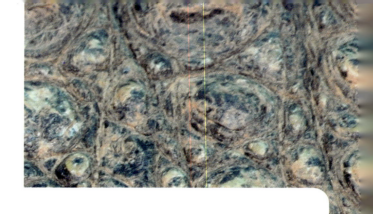

Published by The Child's World®
800-599-READ • www.childsworld.com

Copyright © 2023 by The Child's World®
All rights reserved. No part of this book may be reproduced or utilized in any form or by any means without written permission from the publisher.

Photography Credits
Cover: ©Warpain/Shutterstock; page 1: ©Pan Xunbin/Shutterstock; page 5: ©Warpaint/ Shutterstock; page 6: ©Matt Cardy/Stringer/Getty Images; page 9: ©Ser Amantio di Nicolao/Wikipedia; page 10: ©Elena Duvernay/Stocktrek Images/Getty Images; page 11: ©Andrew Lynchak/Shutterstock; page 12: ©Wlad74/Shutterstock; page 13: ©pxhere; page 14: ©Fred Wieru/Wikipedia; page 15: ©Heritage Images/Contributor/Getty Images; page 16: ©Tuul & Bruno Morandi/Getty Images; page 16: ©Julio Francisco; page 17: ©Julio Francisco; page 19: ©Jeff J Mitchell/Staff/Getty Images; page 21: ©Jane Barlow – PA Images/Contributor/Getty Images

ISBN Information
9781503865297 (Reinforced Library Binding)
9781503865914 (Portable Document Format)
9781503866751 (Online Multi-user eBook)
9781503867598 (Electronic Publication)

LCCN 2022941000
Printed in the United States of America

About the Author

Josh Anderson has published more than 50 books for children and young adults. His two sons, Leo and Dane, are the greatest joys in his life. Josh's hobbies include coaching youth basketball, no-holds-barred games of Exploding Kittens, reading, and family movie nights. His favorite dinosaur is a secret he'll never share!

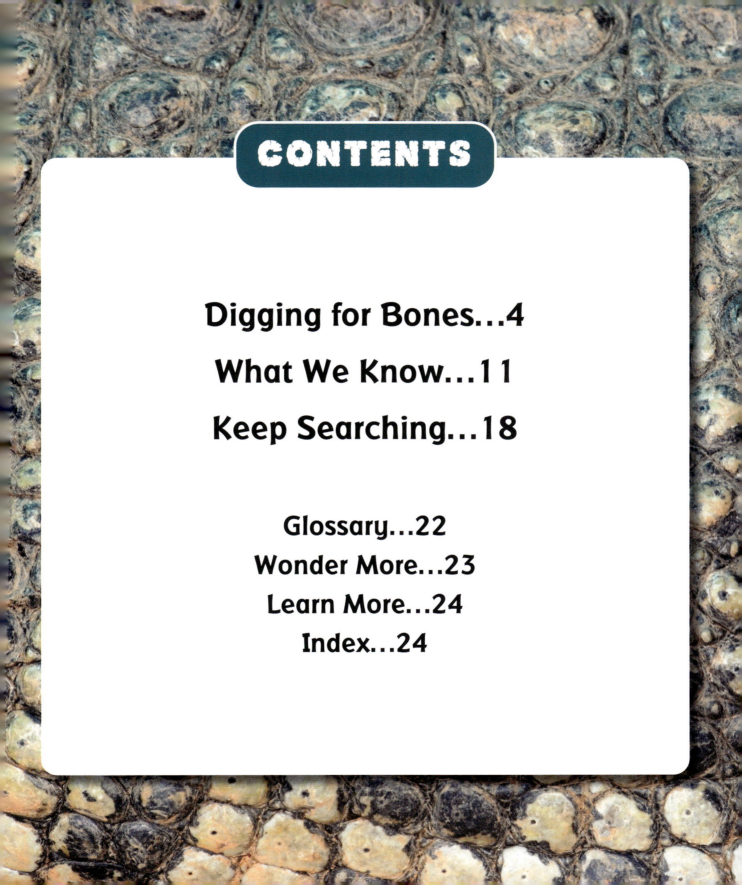

CONTENTS

Digging for Bones...4

What We Know...11

Keep Searching...18

Glossary...22
Wonder More...23
Learn More...24
Index...24

CHAPTER 1

Digging for Bones

Pretend you can time travel to a prehistoric age . . . . You've gone back about 155 million years. You are standing in the low hills of the Rocky Mountains. Suddenly, some birds fly into the air overhead. Something must have spooked them. Then, you see an enormous creature in front of you. It has a long tail and neck. It's a dinosaur called *Diplodocus* (dih-PLAHD-uh-kuss). It is pulling leaves from a large bush. A bird lands on the dinosaur's tail. *Diplodocus* stops eating. It swings its tail hard. The sound it makes is louder than a cannon! You're frozen in place. The terrified bird flies off.

How do we know so much about a creature that lived many millions of years before the first humans? The simple answer: SCIENCE! Let's learn more!

Diplodocus's neck and tail contained around 100 pointy bones known as vertebrae.

Humans have been studying *Diplodocus* for more than 140 years. The first *Diplodocus* **fossils** were found in 1877 near Cañon City, Colorado. Othniel Charles Marsh was the first to study the bones. He was a famous **paleontologist**. Marsh named the creature *Diplodocus*, which means "double beam." Those words describe the shape of the bones underneath the dinosaur's tail.

Diplodocus probably wasn't the longest dinosaur ever to walk the planet. However, it is the longest dinosaur known from a nearly complete skeleton. Other dinosaurs may have been longer. *Supersaurus* (soo–puhr–SAWR–uss) is one example. But those **hypotheses** are based on only partial skeletons.

Scientists have recently learned a lot more about *Diplodocus* teeth. This has helped them learn more about the creature's eating habits.

A 2012 study tried to figure out exactly what *Diplodocus* ate. First, scientists took a **CT scan** of a *Diplodocus* skull. They used that to create a 3D model on a computer. Using the model, they tested how the dinosaur's bones and teeth would have handled different ways of eating.

Scientists used to think *Diplodocus* ate by ripping bark off trees. But the 2012 study raised doubts. That way of eating would've put too much stress on the dinosaur's teeth and skull. Now they think *Diplodocus* probably used its mouth to pull leaves off branches.

Diplodocus teeth broke easily, but they grew back quickly.

A full-grown *Diplodocus* did not have any dinosaur enemies.

CHAPTER 2

What We Know

Diplodocus belonged to a group of dinosaurs called sauropods. All of these creatures had a long neck and tail. But *Diplodocus* might have had the longest tail of all. Some scientists think *Diplodocus* may have weighed more than 20,000 pounds (9,072 kilograms). It was a plant-eater.

When It Lived: 155 million years ago – The Late Jurassic Period
Where It Lived: North America; low hills
First Discovered: 1877, Colorado

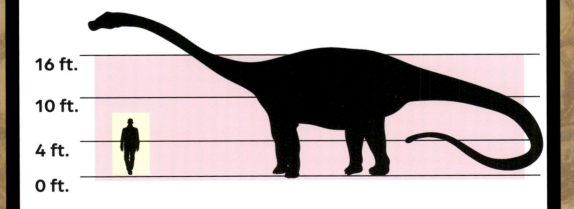

Diplodocus probably needed to eat hundreds of pounds of plant matter each day. A *Diplodocus* herd would quickly eat through an entire area of grasses, shrubs, and trees. The dinosaurs probably spent a lot of time looking for new areas for grazing. *Diplodocus* is thought to have moved a lot like an elephant. Its huge body wasn't built to run. It probably preferred to walk.

FUN FACTS

- The average *Diplodocus* tooth lasted only 35 days. It then fell out and was replaced by a new one.
- Scientists believe *Diplodocus* lived in herds, sleeping and feeding together.
- Scientists used to think *Diplodocus* lived mostly in water. That opinion has changed over time.
- *Diplodocus* hatched from eggs that were probably about the size of a grapefruit.
- Some scientists think that *Diplodocus* could rise up on its back legs to grab something high in the treetops.

THEN AND NOW

For a time, some scientists thought *Diplodocus* had a trunk like an elephant. But a 2006 study helped prove the idea wrong. It compared elephant and *Diplodocus* skulls. Researchers learned *Diplodocus's* head probably couldn't have supported a trunk.

Diplodocus ate at all times of day, stopping to take naps between meals.

Barosaurus likely had the longest neck of any known dinosaur.

Diplodocus wasn't the only long-tailed dinosaur. *Apatosaurus* (uh-pat-oh-SAWR-uss) wasn't quite as long as *Diplodocus*. But it was much heavier. It may have weighed twice as much.

Barosaurus (bayr-oh-SAWR-uss) was longer than *Diplodocus*. It had spines running across its back. Its 30-foot (9.1 m) neck helped it to grab leaves from the treetops. It might have eaten from low shrubs on the ground as well.

Both of these creatures lived at the same time as *Diplodocus*. They lived in the same parts of North America too.

UP FOR DEBATE

In the late 1800s, the two biggest names in paleontology didn't like each other. Edward Drinker Cope and Othniel Charles Marsh engaged in what many have called the "Bone Wars." The men competed against each other to see who could find, research, and name the most new dinosaurs. Their **rivalry** began when Marsh corrected one of Cope's discoveries.

Edward Drinker Cope

DIPLODOCUS
(dih-PLAHD-uh-kuss)

Length: 90 feet (27 m)

Height: 15 feet (4.6 m)

Weight: 24,000 pounds (10,886 kg)

Period: Jurassic

Weakness: Relatively slow-moving; weak bite

Best Defense: Long whip-like tail

ARGENTINOSAURUS
(ar-jehn-tee-noh-SAWR-uss)

Length: 100 feet (30 m)

Height: 70 feet (21 m)

Weight: 200,000 pounds (90,718 kg)

Period: Cretaceous

Weakness: Very slow-moving

Best Defense: Massive size; may be the largest land animal ever discovered

CHAPTER 3

Keep Searching

Scientists are learning new things about dinosaurs every single day. Fossils hold many clues. They even help scientists learn about illnesses dinosaurs might have had!

In 2022, a fossil study from a close relative of *Diplodocus* showed scientists something new. They studied CT scans of a dinosaur nicknamed "Dolly." The scans showed that her neck bones were unusual. Parts of the bones stuck out in odd ways.

These bones would have been connected to Dolly's air sacs. Air sacs were part of a dinosaur's breathing system. Studying **evidence** helped scientists discover that Dolly had had a **respiratory** infection. This was the first time an illness of this kind had been found in a sauropod. The researchers were like time-traveling doctors. They used fossil evidence to identify an illness from about 150 million years ago!

Fossils are the most important tool scientists can use to learn more about dinosaurs.

A nearly complete skull of a young *Diplodocus* was recently discovered. This got scientists excited. The skull was the smallest *Diplodocus* skull ever found. Scientists compared it with the skulls of older *Diplodocus* dinosaurs. The team discovered that the dinosaur's head and teeth changed a lot as *Diplodocus* got older. Scientists started to think about how the dinosaur ate. Since the skulls of the young and older *Diplodocus* were so different, they probably had different diets.

As new tools become available, we can learn much more about these fascinating creatures. Who will make the next big discovery about *Diplodocus* relatives? It could be one of the people reading this book. Maybe you!

The Natural History Museum in London, England, has a life-size model of *Diplodocus* on display. Its name is Dippy, and it has been at the museum since 1905.

GLOSSARY

CT scan (C T SKAN): a more powerful kind of X-ray that shows better detail; CT stands for "computed tomography"

evidence (EV-eh-denss): a clear sign or proof

fossil (FAH-sul): the remains or traces of plants and animals that lived long ago

hypothesis (hy-POTH-eh-sihs): a guess you make based on information you already know

paleontologist (pay-lee-on-TOL-uh-jist): a scientist who studies plants and animals that lived millions of years ago

prehistoric (pree-hiss-TORE-ick): belonging to a period in a time before written history

respiratory (RES-pur-uh-tor-ee): the system of the body that involves breathing

rivalry (RY-vuhl-ree): individuals or groups who strongly compete against each other and often dislike each other

WONDER MORE

Think About It: If you could be any dinosaur for a day, which one would you choose? Why?

Talk About It: You read about the "Bone Wars" on page 15. Ask your family or friends about a time when they were part of a rivalry with another person. How did they resolve the conflict?

Write About It: Take another look at page 4. Write about what it would feel like to travel back in time. What would you be most excited to see? What would you miss most about the present day? Would you go back to the time of the dinosaurs, or is there a different time you'd choose? Explain your answer.

MESOZOIC ERA

Triassic Period
201–252 Million Years Ago

Jurassic Period
145–201 Million Years Ago

Cretaceous Period
66–145 Million Years Ago

LEARN MORE

BOOKS

Carr, Aaron. *Diplodocus*. New York: AV2, 2022.

Finn, Peter. *The Massive Diplodocus*. New York: Enslow Publishing, 2022.

Kelly, Erin Suzanne. *Dinosaurs*. New York: Children's Press, 2021.

WEBSITES

Visit our website for links about *Diplodocus*: **childsworld.com/links**

Note to Parents, Caregivers, Teachers, and Librarians: We routinely verify our web links to make sure they are safe and active sites. So encourage your readers to check them out!

INDEX

air sacs, 18
Apatosaurus, 15
Argentinosaurus, 17

Barosaurus, 15
Bone Wars, 15
bones, 6–8, 18

Cañon City, Colorado, 7

Cope, Edward Drinker, 15

Dolly, 18

illness, 18

leaves, 4, 8, 15

Marsh, Othniel Charles, 7, 15

North America, 11, 15

plant matter, 12

Rocky Mountains, 4

sauropods, 11
Supersaurus, 7

teeth, 8–9